AFRICA

Alexis Roumanis

LET'S READ
AV²
BY WEIGL™
ADDED VALUE • AUDIO VISUAL

Go to **www.av2books.com**, and enter this book's unique code.

BOOK CODE

V669686

AV² by Weigl brings you media enhanced books that support active learning.

AV² provides enriched content that supplements and complements this book. Weigl's AV² books strive to create inspired learning and engage young minds in a total learning experience.

Your AV² Media Enhanced books come alive with...

 Audio
Listen to sections of the book read aloud.

 Video
Watch informative video clips.

 Embedded Weblinks
Gain additional information for research.

 Try This!
Complete activities and hands-on experiments.

 **Key Words**
Study vocabulary, and complete a matching word activity.

 Quizzes
Test your knowledge.

 Slide Show
View images and captions, and prepare a presentation.

... and much, much more!

Published by AV² by Weigl
350 5th Avenue, 59th Floor New York, NY 10118
Websites: www.av2books.com www.weigl.com

Library of Congress Cataloging-in-Publication Data

Roumanis, Alexis, author.
 Africa / Alexis Roumanis.
    pages cm. -- (Exploring continents)
Includes bibliographical references and index.
 ISBN 978-1-4896-3022-3 (hard cover : alk. paper) -- ISBN 978-1-4896-3023-0 (soft cover : alk. paper) --
 ISBN 978-1-4896-3024-7 (single user ebook) -- ISBN 978-1-4896-3025-4 (multi-user ebook)
 1. Africa--Juvenile literature. I. Title.
 DT22.R68 2014
 910.96--dc23
                              2014044121

Printed in the United States of America in Brainerd, Minnesota
1 2 3 4 5 6 7 8 9 0 18 17 16 15 14

122014   Project Coordinator: Jared Siemens
WEP051214   Design: Mandy Christiansen

Weigl acknowledges iStock and Getty Images as the primary image suppliers for this title.

AFRICA

Contents

Welcome to Africa.
It is the second largest continent.

6

This is the shape of Africa. Europe and Asia lie north of Africa. Antarctica sits to the south.

Where Is Africa?

Arctic Ocean

Arctic Ocean

North America

Pacific Ocean

Atlantic Ocean

Europe

Asia

AFRICA

Pacific Ocean

South America

Indian Ocean

N

W   E

S

Antarctica

Two oceans touch the coast of Africa.

Africa is made up of many different landforms. Deserts, mountains, plains, and rainforests can all be found in Africa.

The Sahara Desert is the largest hot desert in the world.

Lake Victoria is the largest lake in Africa.

The Congo rainforest is the largest rainforest in Africa.

Mount Kilimanjaro is Africa's tallest mountain.

The Nile River is the longest river in the world.

Crocodiles have the strongest bite of any animal.

Cheetahs are the fastest land animals in the world.

African elephants are the largest land animals.

Africa is home to some of the world's most unique animals. Many different kinds of animals live there.

Gorillas are the largest apes in the world.

Flamingos are pink because of the food they eat.

Africa is home to many different types of plants.

Nuts from the cola tree are used to make soda.

The baobab tree can keep water in its trunk.

The dragon's blood tree looks like an umbrella.

African grasses can grow
taller than people.

Liana vines can grow
up to 330 feet
(100 meters) long.

Egypt is one of the oldest countries in Africa. It is more than 6,000 years old. People have lived in Africa for thousands of years.

The Maasai are one of the first peoples of Africa.

Many kinds of people live in Africa. Each group of people is special in its own way.

Maasai warriors often wear colorful jewelry.

Men in Nigeria often wear loose robes called agbadas.

Some Ethiopian women color their hair with red soil and butter.

Women in Kenya wear beads to show they are married.

More than 1.1 billion people live in Africa. The country with the most land in Africa is Algeria.

The city with the most people in Africa is Lagos, Nigeria.

There are many things that can be found only in Africa. People come from all over the world to visit this continent.

Victoria Falls is the largest waterfall in the world.

People go on safaris to see animals in nature.

People can see 10 countries by taking a boat down the Nile River.

Thousands of people visit the
Great Pyramids of Giza
every day.

The Great Wildebeest Migration of
the Serengeti is the world's largest
movement of animals.

21

Africa Quiz

See what you have learned about the continent of Africa.

What do these pictures tell you about Africa?

23

KEY WORDS

Research has shown that as much as 65 percent of all written material published in English is made up of 300 words. These 300 words cannot be taught using pictures or learned by sounding them out. They must be recognized by sight. This book contains 80 common sight words to help young readers improve their reading fluency and comprehension. This book also teaches young readers several important content words, such as proper nouns. These words are paired with pictures to aid in learning and improve understanding.

Page	Content Words First Appearance	Page	Content Words First Appearance
4	is, it, second, the, to	4	Africa, continent
7	and, of, this, two, where	7	Antarctica, Asia, coast, Europe, oceans
8	all, be, can, different, found, in, made, many, mountains, up, world	8	Congo, deserts, lake, landforms, plains, rainforests
9	river	10	bite, cheetahs, crocodiles, elephants
10	animals, any, are, have, land	11	apes, flamingos, gorillas
11	because, eat, food, home, kinds, live, most, some, there, they	12	cola, nuts, soda, trunk, umbrella
12	an, from, its, keep, like, looks, make, plants, tree, water	13	grasses, vines
13	feet, grow, long, people, than	15	Egypt, Maasai
15	first, for, more, old, years	16	jewelry, men, Nigeria, robes, warriors
16	each, group, often, own, way	17	beads, butter, hair, Kenya, soil, women
17	show, their, with	19	Algeria, Lagos
19	city, country	20	boat, nature, safaris, waterfall
20	a, by, come, down, go, on, only, over, see, things	21	migration, movement, pyramids, wildebeest
21	day, every, great